kids'
container
gardening

kids' container gardening

Year-round projects for inside and out

by Cindy Krezel

Photography by Bruce Curtis

 Ball Publishing | Chicago

Ball Publishing
An imprint of Chicago Review Press, Incorporated
814 North Franklin Street
Chicago, IL 60610
www.ballpublishing.com

Library of Congress Cataloging-in-Publication Data

Krezel, Cindy.

  Kids' container gardening : year-round projects for inside and out / by
Cindy Krezel ; photography by Bruce Curtis.
     p. cm.
  ISBN 978-1-883052-75-1
  1. Container gardening—Juvenile literature. 2. Children's
gardens—Juvenile literature. 3. Gardening—Experiments—Juvenile
literature. 4. Gardening—Study and teaching—Activity programs—Juvenile
literature. I. Curtis, Bruce, ill. II. Title.

  SB418.K77 2005
  635.9'86—dc22

                    2005002543

This book was printed and bound in November 2009 for Imago USA in Heyuan, Guangdong, China.
10   123456789

ISBN 978-1-883052-75-1

This book is for my sister, Kyria—first reader and

editor, job counselor, great friend, and dinner

companion, with much love.

contents

Garden
Aquariums
page 49

acknowledgements

First, I want to thank Bruce Curtis for walking up to me at Arbor Day and saying, "I have a book I want you to write." As it turns out, it was a book I wanted to write, too. Many thanks to Ellen Talmage, for her guidance and for passing the baton so generously, and to Rick Blanchette for being the kindest of editors to a new author. Many thanks to Estelle and to Joan, who kept me on my path. But most of all I want to thank all of the great kids who make up this book: Taylor, Leon, Alex and Wil (even though I know it was your mom's idea), Curtis, Kevin, Danny and Mario (the best neighbors ever!), Sheila, Troy, Scott, Katie, Erin and Tara (who came to my rescue not once but twice), Jonathan, and as always, my sister, Kyria, who's come to my rescue too often to count.

Thank you all a kazillion times!

A Few Words for Grown-ups about Gardening with Children

introduction

Gardening gets you in touch with the earth. It's good for the soul. It's especially good for children, who have so little control over their own daily lives. Playing God in the garden and learning that our actions can affect the world around us is an important lesson to learn at any age. Gardening with children, in my opinion, is also the best kind of quality time. Ask anyone who gardened with a grandparent. Watch the look on their face as they talk about their memories.

Ask your little ones if they'd like a garden of their own. It doesn't have to be big. A garden in a martini glass, a salad bowl, a hanging basket for the porch—all are great ways to start. Give children the supplies they need and then let them go. Who cares if they get it "right"? Plants are amazingly forgiving. Even killing a plant can be an adventure and a learning experience. And when kids do it well, seeing something they planted themselves actually grow can be the beginning of a lifelong love and a source of memories for a lifetime.

Sharing this experience with someone makes a lasting impact not only on children but on your relationship with those children. I'm sure you'll agree— it's well worth the effort.

And it's a lot of fun!

before you start

chapter 1

There are things plants need to grow.

If we know them and plan—and plant!—

accordingly, our plants will be happy,

and so will we. If we try to cut corners

and do what's easy for us but not best for

the plants, we won't have great looking

gardens. And since we garden for the

fun of it, why not do it right?

Find out about the plants you choose. Find out what they like. Then see to it that these needs are filled. You wouldn't send your little sister out into the cold without a coat or forget to feed the dog, would you? Plants tell you what they want in quiet ways. They wilt or turn colors or the leaves curl up or shrivel. You have to watch carefully. If you do, your plants will tell you how they feel.

Also, if you're planting two or more plants together, make sure they like the same things. A shade plant that needs a lot of water and one that needs dry soil and sun will never do well in the same container. Get to know the plants you choose and plant them with their "friends," those who like the same conditions.

Roots need water and food, just like people. Some need more, some need less. Some can stand in water, others need almost totally dry soil, with an occasional dunk. Plants will tell you if they are getting enough, not enough, or too much water, if you pay attention to them. Pay attention. Your plants depend on you. They can't run away.

The signs of too much and not enough water can look the same if you only look at the leaves. If the leaves wilt or curl up, check the soil. Feel the soil every day or two. Is it wet? Is it dry? Does the soil smell rotten? If you need help finding out what is wrong, ask a person who works at a garden center.

You also have to be very careful when handling your plants. Never hold a plant by the stem, leaves, or flowers. Always hold it by the roots or by the pot. A plant can be removed from the pot by tipping it on its side or slightly upside down and then knocking gently or pushing from the bottom and freeing it. Then hold it by the roots when planting.

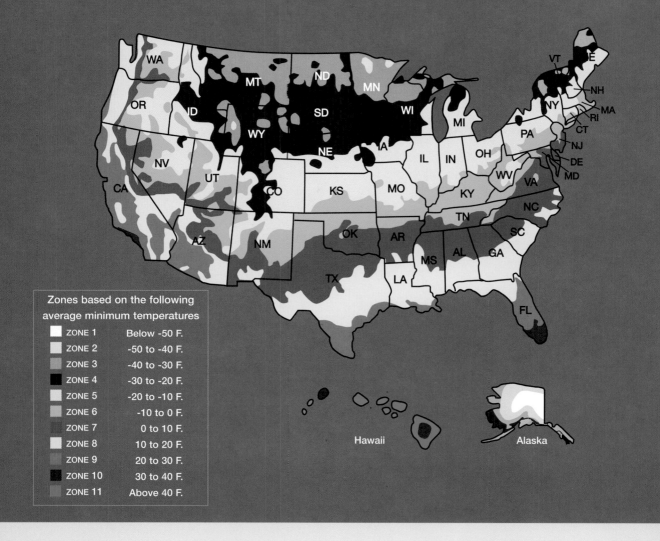

Zones based on the following
average minimum temperatures

	ZONE 1	Below -50 F.
	ZONE 2	-50 to -40 F.
	ZONE 3	-40 to -30 F.
	ZONE 4	-30 to -20 F.
	ZONE 5	-20 to -10 F.
	ZONE 6	-10 to 0 F.
	ZONE 7	0 to 10 F.
	ZONE 8	10 to 20 F.
	ZONE 9	20 to 30 F.
	ZONE 10	30 to 40 F.
	ZONE 11	Above 40 F.

Something else to think about is how cold it gets in your area. It won't matter for indoor plants, but if your containers will be left outside, it's good to know what "Zone" you're in. The USDA Zone Map tells you how cold different parts of the United States get. Find where you are, what Zone number you live in, and choose plants that have your Zone number or a higher (warmer) number. Here is the Zone Map. Can you find where you are and what zone you're in?

You also want to wait until after the last danger of frost before you plant certain plants. Find out when your town's frost-free date is, and don't plant anything delicate outside until after it is past.

When planning a planting, one way to design is with a color wheel. Color wheels show the full range of colors and how they blend into one another. Below are the three "color concepts" used when planning a garden. They are big words, but you will easily understand them, especially when you see them.

Each of these will give a planting a different "feel." Try holding pots of plants next to each other to see how you like them. Then plant whatever you like the best (as long as the plants have the same needs). Pick colors that make you feel good or that you really like!

Here are a few things you don't usually think about: sunscreen, water, and bug spray. Pretty exciting stuff, huh? But they can be the difference between a great experience and a horrible one. If you are working outside for any amount of time, be sure to plan ahead. Put on sunscreen, bring water to drink, and carry bug spray if needed. Better to have it and not need it than need it and not have it, as my mother always says. (And she's almost always right!)

Monochromatic: This is using all one color, like using many different plants that are all white or all have red flowers.

Analogous: This is using colors that are similar or blend into one another, like pink, lavender, and purple.

Complementary: This is using colors on opposite sides of the color wheel, so the colors are very different, like yellow and purple, or green and red.

must-have supplies

Maybe these are not things you must have, but I always end up using them when I make garden projects, whether with kids or for myself. Keep them around so that when the spirit moves you, you're ready to garden.

Peat pellets

Silly that they should be indispensable, but to me they are. I use them in the bottoms of terrariums, as seed starters and…well, you'll see. I use them a lot. Order them online or buy a bunch next time you're in a garden center, and store them in a Ziploc bag. They really come in handy.

Old pots

Always save old pots, of whatever size. Use broken shards at the bottom of planters. Use them whole as the makings of pot people (See pages 27–30). Start plants in them any time. Old pots are better than having to buy new!

Bagged potting soil

I hate the word *never* and almost always try whatever I'm told never to do. But this is one thing that I really never do: Never dig soil out of the garden for new container plantings. It just doesn't work. Whether germs in the dirt make the plants sick or the soil just isn't good for planters, it's not worth the effort to start new plants in old soil. Start right, and you will be successful. You'll be glad you did.

Ok, now you're ready to garden. On your mark, get set…go!

starting in spring

chapter 2

Take-out Seed Start Greenhouses

Don't throw away those plastic take-out trays you get from restaurants! They make great "incubator" greenhouses. Plant seeds in them, then when your plants have sprouted, transplant the baby plants outside into the garden or pots. This is an easy way to start annual flowers or vegetables early in the season for a longer lasting garden.

WHAT TO DO | Take-out Seed Start Greenhouses

1. **Be sure that the take-out container is clean and dry.** Run it through the dishwasher or wash and dry it well by hand.

2. **Set the lid off to the side and put the take-out container on a table or flat surface.** Put in as many peat pellets as will fit side by side with no overlap, or as many as you want to start. If you look closely at the pellets, you will see a bottom and a "top," with a circle and a dot in the center. The top goes up.

    Add enough warm water to cover the pellets, filling the container about two-thirds of the way. Some of the pellets will float to the top. That's OK. If the water is warm, they will begin to expand almost immediately. It's fun to watch them. First they look like small Oreo cookies. Then they swell, getting fatter and wetter all the time. In about 2 to 10 minutes they will be "done," depending on how warm the water is. They will be 2–3 inches tall, soft and plump, with a hole in the top. If all the water has been absorbed and the pellets aren't all the way open, add a little more water. If there is leftover water in the container and the pellets are completely open, carefully pour out the extra water. Now you are ready to plant your seeds.

WHAT YOU NEED

✓ Plastic take-out tray

✓ Peat pellets

✓ Warm water

✓ Seeds

✓ Plant stakes or short popsicle sticks

3. **Write the name of each kind of seed onto a plant label.** Push the label down into the pellet at the outside of the hole. Do this until each pellet has a label for the kind of seed you will be putting there.

4. **Take a plant label out of one of the pellets.** Carefully open that packet of seeds and push two to four seeds down into the pellet until they are partly buried in the peat moss. Replace the plant label. Do this with each kind of seed until all of the pellets have seeds. Now push the labels back down into the pellets, so they are in firmly.

5. **Set the lid on the take-out tray.** The labels should prevent it from closing completely, which is just fine. You want the lid of the tray to hold moisture in while still letting in air from the outside. If you can see condensation (water beads, or trapped moisture) on the inside of the lid, it is a good sign.

6. **Now put the tray inside the house in a bright, warm window.** Each day, take the lid off the tray and look at the plants. In seven to ten days you will see little sprouts growing. Once they are as tall as the top of the container, take the top off. Now you will have to check carefully for water. They may need to be watered every day, or every few days, depending on how hot and dry your house is. The pellets can't sit in standing water, but they can't dry out either. Watch them carefully. You have little baby plants to care for!

7. **Leave your little pellet babies in the tray for no more than two to three weeks or else they will get long and leggy.** Peat pellets, though a great way to start plants, have no natural nutrients, so you want to get the plants into the ground and fertilized as soon as possible. Depending on what zone you are in (see the chart on page 3), you can put your little pellet babies out into the garden after the last chance of frost. They can

continued on page 10 ▶

WHAT TO DO | Take-out Seed Start Greenhouses *(continued)*

go into the ground or into large pots. Whichever you do, add lots of organics, such as compost and composted manure when you plant. Make a hole just slightly wider and just as deep as the pellet. Gently rip the mesh of the pellet open, but don't try to take the plant out. Simply set the whole pellet into the ground and push the soil back up against it. You've planted your pellets!

Be sure to watch and water your plants once they are in the ground. This is a great way to start your yearly vegetable or flower garden.

WHAT TO DO | Great Big Garden Bowls for Mom

This is the favorite project of many of my favorite kids. It feels wonderful to give

Mom a great big bowl of flowers for Mother's Day that will flower all season long.

What better way to say "I love you, Mom"?

1. Fill your planter with soil to 3 inches below the top. Pat the soil down gently with your fingers so it is flat and even. Enjoy the feel of the soil!

2. Now pick the flowers that you want to put into your pot. How big the plants and your pot are will determine how many plants you can put into your pot. Don't put them too close together! Annual plants can triple in size in a season, so you want to leave at least as much space between plants as the plants are now.

WHAT YOU NEED

✓ A big pot or salad bowl, with a drainage hole in the bottom

✓ Potting soil

✓ Some annual flowers in cell packs. It's a lot of fun to go to the garden center and pick flowers with Dad or Mom. See the list of flowers on page 13, but there are many other choices!

✓ A watering can or cups full of water

WHAT TO DO | Great Big Garden Bowls for Mom *(continued)*

3. Take a minute to read the labels or signs on the plants you choose. **Make sure the plants you pick will be "friends."** If you put a shade-loving plant in a pot with a sun lover, one of them won't be happy. Pick plants that are compatible in terms of their water and sun needs, so you can keep your plants happy and healthy.

4. **When you pick up a plant, never hold it by the stems, leaves, or flowers.** Only hold it by the roots. Plants have veins, just like people, and they are very delicate. If you bruise a plant, you may not see the bruise, but it will wilt and eventually die. So always hold plants by their roots. If you need to, turn the container over and let the plant slide into your hand. Then, have a look at it. This is the only chance during the life of the plant that you will get to look at the whole thing—roots, stems, and all. Have a good look. Isn't it cool? Are the roots very noticeable around the outside of the root ball? If so, it's probably because the roots have been trying to grow outward and kept hitting the plastic container. Very, very gently pull as many of them out as you can and spread them out when you plant. "Unsnarling" these roots, even if you break a few of them, will help the plant grow better in the long run. When you are done admiring the roots, set the plants you've chosen onto the bed of soil.

5. **Fill in around the plants with as many small handfuls of soil as it takes.** Don't cover higher than where the roots and the stems join. That's called the "crown" of the plant. You should never bury a plant deeper than that, or you will smother the plant.

6. **Now gently pour water over your fingers and down onto the planter bowl.** Your fingers will break the fall of the water and direct it where it's needed.

7. **Did you remember to find out about your plants when you picked them?** Do they like sun or shade? Place your planter wherever your plants prefer. Water only as often as needed. Take one finger, every day, and touch your soil. If it's dry to the touch and the plants seem to sag, water the bowl. If not, wait and check again the next day.

8. **Your flowers will get bigger and bigger and will flower all the way until the frost.**

This is great for Mom, Grandma, or anyone else you want to remind every day that you love them!

Some fun annuals for planters:
Sun lovers: ageratum, celosia, dusty miller, *Gomphrena*, lantana, geraniums, marigolds, New Guinea impatiens, petunias, *Scaevola*, verbena

Shade lovers: Begonias, caladium, coleus, impatiens, *Mimulus* (also called monkey flower—what a silly name!), *Torenia*

📋 WHAT TO DO | Vegetable Hanging Baskets

This is a great end-of-school teacher gift or something fun to hang around the house and harvest (that means pop in your mouth!) as you pass by.

1. **Make sure your planter has drain holes.** If necessary, have a parent punch a few holes in the bottom. Add enough soil to the pot so that the soil comes to about 3–4 inches below the rim.

2. **Now gently take three basil plants out of the cell pack.** Center them as a triangle in the center of the pot. Take out three marigolds. Set them slightly outside and between the basil. Now take out three tomato plants. Set them at the outer edge, around the marigolds.

☑ WHAT YOU NEED

✓ A pot, at least 10 inches across, that can be hung (hangers attached or with a separate hanger)

✓ An organic-rich potting soil, preferably with some compost in it

✓ One cell-pack* of cherry tomatoes (use only cherry tomatoes, which will hang down)

✓ One cell-pack* of basil

✓ One cell-pack* of marigolds

A cell-pack is the way baby plants are sold in the spring. There are usually four plants to a pack. This is the perfect size to start your little garden.

WHAT TO DO | Vegetable Hanging Baskets *(continued)*

3. **Gently open all of the roots and set them firmly onto the soil.** Now add soil up to the crown of the plants. Tuck it in with your fingers so the plants are nicely secure in the soil.

4. **Water gently with a soft spray of water so the plants don't get moved.** You want them to settle in. You are ready now to give your gift if you are making it for someone or to hang it if you are keeping it.

5. **Since these are vegetables, your planter will need to go in full sun and be watered whenever it feels dry.** Don't let it stay wet (that's why you need the holes), but don't let the leaves wilt from thirst either. Watch your planter and touch a finger to the soil every day, and you will get to know how often it needs to be watered.

6. **The basil can be picked as soon as it has at least six leaves.** Take no more than one-third of the leaves at a time. Pick leaves from the bottom of the plant. Be sure to pinch off any flower buds that form on the basil. Once it makes flowers, the leaves become bitter.

MORE ABOUT VEGETABLE HANGING BASKETS

Cool Facts

Why did we plant marigolds with our basil and tomatoes? Two reasons: 1. Marigolds are pretty and they flower all summer long. 2. Marigolds have a chemical in them called pyrethrin, which smells bad to insects. So they help to keep away bad bugs. Since we will be eating some of what we grow, we want to use only healthy organics if we possibly can. Marigolds help us to do that!

Father's Day Fountains

This is one to do with an adult because you use tools and electricity. It takes a little work and a few special supplies, but when you're done, you have a fountain! That works! That you made together! How cool is that?

✅ WHAT YOU NEED

✓ A large (at least 12 inches across) flat, waterproof container with no holes in the bottom. You can use a villa pot, an old wagon, or anything else you can come up with. If it has a plugged hole, you may be able to caulk it with bathroom caulking. If you do, be sure to let the caulk "cure" and harden according to the instructions.

✓ A tabletop fountain pump. This can be found at any good garden center or pond supply or online. Tell them how large the container is or how many gallons of water and how high you want it to pump. They should be able to tell you the right size. If you do not know how big it will be, you should be OK with a number 60 or 80 tabletop fountain pump.

✓ Pretty rocks, enough to cover the bottom of the container to a depth of 1–2 inches

✓ One clay pot, with a hole in the bottom, large enough to stand as high as you want your fountain and proportional to the larger container

✓ One piece of tubing, to go from the pump top to the top of the fountain. Buy 1–2 feet, to be safe.

✓ Two or three pieces of slate. Roofing slate is great, and most roofing supply stores will sell you (or even give you) just a piece or two. Ask for broken pieces. But be careful! They may be sharp.

✓ A drill and a ¾-inch drill bit.

✓ One or more water plants, in 4-inch pots. My favorite for this is the peace lily, or spathophyllum, but you can use whatever you like.

📋 WHAT TO DO | **Father's Day Fountains** (continued)

1. **Getting the supplies gathered is the hardest part, I promise!** Once you have them, you're ready to make a fountain.

2. **Check to make sure the container is waterproof.** If not, you'll need to use a different one.

3. **Take the slate that you will use as your main piece and soak it in water while you do the next steps.** It will be easier to drill if you do.

4. **Next, take the pump out of its box.** Test it in some water. *Be careful!* Pumps use water and electricity. They are not to be fooled around with. Never touch the plug with wet hands or get water near the electrical outlet.

5. **Attach the tubing to the out end of the pump.** Thread the tubing up through the clay pot, which should be turned upside down. Set it aside.

6. **Now fill the bottom of the large pot with clean, pretty rocks.** Set the pump/tube/clay pot unit onto the rocks, about a third of the way from whatever will be the "back" of the fountain. Make sure there are enough rocks beneath it that water can get in to the pump.

7. **Thread the electric cord to the "back" of the fountain and up and out.** Use a small piece of duct tape to fasten it to the sidewall. Take a water plant and set it into the rocks over the cord, to hide the cord from view. A rock or two against the pot should hold it in place.

8. Take the piece of slate out of the water. For safety, wear a pair of safety gloves and goggles for this step. Cut a piece of slate big enough to cover the top of the pot but small enough that it's smaller than your container. The slate can be broken over the edge of a table or with a screwdriver and a hammer till you have the size you want. Be careful! Break gently or it will shatter and the edges will be very sharp where it breaks. With a ¾-inch bit on the drill, drill a hole where you want the water to come through. Be sure to save the leftover pieces of slate.

9. Thread the tubing through the hole in the slate so the slate sits atop the upside-down pot. Cut the tube off just above the slate. Fill the basin a third to halfway full of water.

10. DRY OFF YOUR HANDS! Plug the electric cord into an outlet. Water should pump up through the tube and pour out over the slate, then fall back into the pot, and go back through the filter. If it doesn't, unplug the pump before you investigate!

11. Now arrange the leftover slate over the hole. You can get the water to do lots of different things depending on how you block or cover the tubing. Use small pieces of slate to get it to do what you want. If you are adding more plants to the basin, do it now. Otherwise, shake your adult's hand and enjoy your fountain!

You can get the water to do lots of different things depending on how you block or cover the tubing.

simmering summer

Butterfly Gardens

Butterflies make a garden joyful. They're so graceful and delicate. All it takes to attract butterflies to your yard are a few simple things—sunlight,colorful flowers, and some plants for their babies. Here's how to make a garden both you and the butterflies will love.

chapter 3

📝 WHAT TO DO | Butterfly Gardens

1. **Decide where to put your butterfly garden.** It must be a hot, sunny place. Butterflies are ectotherms, which means they need the sun to warm them up so they can fly. The plants they sip from are all sun-lovers too, so pick a bright, sunny spot for your butterfly garden.

2. **Put some soil in the bottom of the pot.** Leave enough room for the plants' roots plus 1 to 1½ inches empty at the top (so when you water, the soil and water stay in the pot).

3. **Decide how many plants you want to put into your planter and where you want them.** The best way to do this is to set the plants, pots and all, on the bed of soil. Move them around until you like the way they look. Leave room in the arrangement for the pie tin, laid flat and set into the soil.

4. **Take the plants out of the pots and plant them into the soil.** Fill in around them with soil and tuck it in with your fingers to fill in all the spaces.

📋 WHAT YOU NEED

✓ An unused sandbox or an old tire is ideal, but any large flat box, crate, or tub will work nicely

✓ One pie tin, preferably aluminum

✓ Lots of potting soil

✓ Some gravel or small rocks

✓ A watering can and water

✓ As many butterfly-attracting plants as will fit with room to grow (on page 26)

5. **Set the pie tin into the soil up to the rim.** Fill it halfway with gravel or rocks, then fill the tin with water.

6. **Water the whole container gently, to soak and settle the plants.** Don't forget to check it often. Plants in full sun dry out quickly! Also, fill the tin with water.

Now walk away and wait for the butterflies to come!

continued on page 26

Decide where to put your butterfly garden. It must be a hot, sunny place.

🔍 MORE ABOUT BUTTERFLY GARDENS (continued)

Butterflies

What attracts butterflies? They are attracted to flowers for three qualities:

1. **Shape.** Butterflies sip nectar through a long, hollow tongue. They need strong stems to perch on.

2. **Color.** Butterflies see the full range of colors. Not even humans can do that!

3. **Fragrance.** Butterflies have a wonderful sense of smell, so the more good-smelling flowers you plant, the easier it is for them to find your garden.

Butterflies love to sip these plants. Annuals: asters, cosmos, dahlias, heliotrope, lantana, marigolds, nasturtium, petunias, snapdragon, verbena, zinnia. **Perennials:** butterfly weed (*Asclepias*), hollyhocks, Joe Pye weed, monarda.

Caterpillars

Don't forget to take care of "baby" butterflies—caterpillars! Be sure to include some plants for caterpillars to eat. If you include plants for this larval stage, then butterflies will stay in your yard longer and then lay their eggs right onto the leaves of plants like parsley, dill, or carrots. When the eggs hatch, caterpillars will come out and eat the leaves until they're ready to form a chrysalis before turning into butterflies. It will all happen right in your yard!

Plant these plants for caterpillars to eat: parsley, dill, carrots, chives, hollyhocks, lupines, nettle, sage.

WHAT TO DO | Pot People

Every garden needs some little folk to watch over it. Pot people are friendly and kind and grow with your garden. Add one to your windowsill or garden—you'll enjoy the company!

1. **First, lay out all of the pieces and make sure you have everything you need.** There's nothing worse than getting started and finding you have to stop because you're missing something.

WHAT YOU NEED

✓ Six small clay pots with holes in the bottom (I used 2-inch pots)

✓ One clay orchid pot with slits in the sides and a hole in the bottom, 2–3 times bigger than the first pots (I used a 6-inch pot)

✓ One "in-between" sized classic clay pot (I used a 4-inch pot)

✓ Craft cord, as is used to braid ankle bracelets, 1–2 yards

✓ Five beads or stringable balls, each larger than the hole in the bottom of the pots

✓ One pair of googly eyes and craft glue, and/or waterproof paints to paint a face

✓ Potting soil or peat pellet

✓ Grass seed

📋 WHAT TO DO | Pot People *(continued)*

2. Next, stack two sets of two small pots and set the pots upside down. Cut two pieces of craft cord twice as long as the largest pot. Make a knot and tie a bead onto one end of each cord. String the bead up into the bottom, open end of one set of two pots and up, so it extends out the small hole. Do this with each set, so you now have two "legs."

3. Tie the two cords together, about halfway up the cord that's showing, but don't tie a bead there. String the large orchid pot, upside down, onto the craft cord, so the cord extends up through the small hole in the top. The "legs" will probably fit under it.

4. Take the in-between sized pot and put it right side up on top of the orchid pot. String the double cord up through the top. Holding it carefully, move the cord up and down, so you can see how long you want the legs to be under the body, once you tie the top knot. When you have the right size, (remembering that you have to tie "high" and then it will drop to the bottom of the pot once you let go), tie a bead into the double cord and cut off any extra cord. You now have a body, legs, and a head.

5. Cut a piece of craft cord that is about 1½ times as big as the orchid pot. Tie a bead onto one end and string one pot on. Run the cord from one side to the other of the orchid pot. You may have to put your hand inside from the bottom to guide it through. String the last small pot on the other side (small side to the body, open side out) and pull it a little tight. Measure how long you want the "arms" once you tie the knot. When you have the length you want, tie a bead onto the cord and cut off any extra cord. You have arms!

6. **I like a simple look, but you can make your pot people as elaborate as you want.** Glue simple googly eyes, or paint the whole thing. It's up to you! (Be sure he's dry before you put him outside.)

7. **Fill the top pot with soil or drop in an expanded peat pellet.** Press grass seed into the soil.

8. **Place your little friend in a sunny spot.** Keep his head well watered and in a few days you will see him sprout a head of grassy "hair." Keep it watered and enjoy! Once you see how the grass grows, you can try different seeds to give your pot person fun or "seasonal" hairdos. Use seeds for herbs or low-growing flowers. **Have fun!**

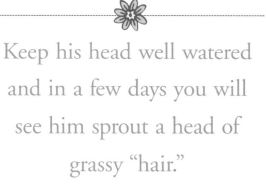

Keep his head well watered and in a few days you will see him sprout a head of grassy "hair."

WHAT TO DO | Salad Bowls

There's nothing like a salad picked fresh from the garden—especially if you grew it all yourself. Salad bowls are so simple and so much fun to grow! These can be planted any time of the year and kept inside or out, but my favorite time to plant one is the middle of summer. Any good garden center will have vegetable seeds until early fall. Midsummer is a great time to plant a crop of vegetables for fall. A nice lettuce mix, such as mesclun or mâche mix, will give you lots of colors.

1. Make sure there are holes in the bottom of the bowl, or make a layer of broken pottery or packing peanuts on the bottom to give you drainage.
2. Fill the bowl with potting soil to about 1 inch below the top of the bowl.

WHAT YOU NEED

✓ A big salad bowl you don't use any big bowl, or a basket lined with plastic

✓ Potting soil

✓ Seeds for lettuce

✓ A watering can

WHAT TO DO | Salad Bowls (continued)

3. **Spread a fine layer of seeds across the top of the soil.** Try to spread them apart so they don't grow on top of one another.

4. **Water gently with a soft spray of water so that you soak the soil nicely without making holes in the soil or moving the seed around with the force of the water.**

5. **Put your pot in a bright sunny place, either inside or out.** Every day touch the soil gently. If it's dry, water just enough to wet the surface, without drowning the baby plants.

6. **Once your little plants have three leaves, you can begin to harvest lettuce.** You may pick one out of every three, as the plant grows bigger. Since you've planted lots of little baby plants, you will be able to pick a few leaves every day, maybe even enough to make a little fresh salad!

7. **Once the weather gets cold enough to freeze, or when the plant suddenly sends up a stalk, you won't be able to pick any more.** Turn the bowl upside down into the compost pile and dig it in. You can start another one for inside the house if you want, but clean the bowl thoroughly and start with all new potting soil.

Worm Boxes

Kids often love the gross and icky in the garden

even more than they love the pretty and sweet.

So I encourage them! Grown-ups may be scared or

grossed out by worms, but once you understand

how lovable they are, you'll be their friend

for life!

WHAT YOU NEED

✓ A plastic sweater box or flat-bottomed container, at least 5 inches deep, with a lid

✓ Old newspaper

✓ Some soil from the garden (not potting soil)

✓ Leftover plant material from the kitchen (see Worm Diet on page 36)

✓ A spray bottle with plain water for misting

✓ Worms! Red wigglers are best, though night crawlers and earthworms are fine and usually easier to find. These can be found in the garden, at a local bait shop, or ordered online.

WHAT TO DO | Worm Boxes (continued)

1. **Ask a grown up to punch small air holes in the lid of your worm box.**

2. **Take one sheet of newspaper to fit on the bottom.** Now tear (don't cut—worms can get paper cuts from the sharp edges) enough newspaper to make a soft "bed" about one inch deep in the box. Slightly crunch the newspaper so it doesn't lay flat but has lots of air and "cushion" to it.

3. **Sprinkle about 1–1½ inches of soil on top.** Gently tap the box so the soil settles into the paper.

4. **Spray lightly with water.** You don't want to soak the soil, just give it some moisture. If the soil was already moist, you may be able to skip this step. But if the soil was dry, give it a few good spritzes.

5. **Now gently set a few worms into your worm box.** Don't be afraid. They may wiggle a little when you pick them up, but they don't bite or do anything scary. They're more afraid of you than you can possibly be of them. So be nice to them!

6. **Take a little bit of the food scraps you've saved and sprinkle them on the top.** Don't squish your worms with food. Give them just a little. If you have about an inch of space left at the top of your box it's perfect.

7. **Now put the lid securely onto the top of your worm box.** It needs to go in a cool, dark place. Under the kitchen sink works nicely, or even under your bed. But don't be surprised if mom vetoes both of these ideas. If she does, know that she isn't over her fear of worms—unlike you!—and look for another place. You can put your worm box in a cool, shady spot in the garden or garage.

However, your worm box can't ever be in the direct sun. Worms (who live underground) can't tolerate bright light, and the heat of the sun on the box will kill them.

8. **Check on your worms every day.** They will eat the food you give them and turn it into "worm castings," the clumpy brown soil you will begin to see in your box. Make sure there is moisture without the box filling with water. You can look at the side of the box to see if there is sitting water. Dump it out if there is because worms will drown. Once a month, turn the box upside down in the compost pile or garden. Leave it for a few minutes, then lift the top layer off and put it back into your box. The worms will have wriggled to the top. Add more paper and start again. You will have a garden full of worms and healthy soil in no time. And you will have enjoyed the company of worms!

continued on page 36 ▶

You can put your worm box in a cool, shady spot in the garden or garage. However, your worm box can't ever be in the direct sun. Worms (who live underground) can't tolerate bright light, and the heat of the sun on the box will kill them.

Cool Facts about Worms

When you take out your worms, gently hold one in the palm of your hand. The worm will feel your body's heat and begin to move around. That's because worms are cold-blooded, or ectothermic, just like butterflies. They can't create their own heat, like we do.

Look closely at your worm. Take a look at its many segments. It may have a slightly wider, lighter colored band in the middle of its body. This is called the clitellum and is where the worm has its eggs. Worms are both boys and girls at the same time. They can all make eggs. Worms come to the surface of the soil during rain to meet other worms. It's easier for them to move in the rain, so they are more active. Unfortunately, they can get caught on the sidewalk or road once the sun comes out. When I see a marooned worm, I like to pick it up and put in back in the ground. They do so much for us, I think it's the least I can do for them!

It's time to clear up a worm myth. If you cut a worm in half, it will not live as two worms! Worms can grow a new tail end if it's cut off, but the worm must have been cut at least 10 segments after the clitellum to survive. If it does, the front will live and grow a new tail, but the back will still die.

Worm Diet

Things to feed worms: potato peelings, coffee grounds, orange peels (cut small), bread, apple cores. **Things to not feed worms:** butter, animal fat, meat, eggshells, cheese.

fall

favorites

Cocktail Gardens

This is a really fun project to do at home, but be careful—a few moisture crystals go a loooong way! Making cuttings of plants is easy, and it's fun to see roots grow.

chapter 4

37

WHAT TO DO | Cocktail Gardens

1. **Fill the glass you picked halfway with water.** Now pour the water into a measuring cup. How much water do you have?

2. **Look on the package of moisture crystals.** Ask a grown-up to help you figure out how many crystals you need for the amount of water you have. Don't use more than the package says!

3. **Measure the crystals into your glass and add the water from the measuring cup.** Set it aside until the crystals have absorbed all of the moisture.

4. **When the crystals are soft and gel-like, hold some in your hands.** Isn't it weird? The gel in the glass should feel like Jell-O, firm enough to hold a piece of plant up but still moist enough that water is available to the cutting.

5. **If you want, add a few drops of food coloring and stir it with a spoon** (you'll dye your hands if you touch it). It will dye the plant but is pretty.

6. **Have a grownup help you take a cutting of a plant you want to root.** Use a clean, sharp knife or pruner. Trim the leaves off so the bottom 2–3 inches of stem are bare.

WHAT YOU NEED

✓ A clear, interesting-shaped glass, like a giant martini, margarita, or champagne glass

✓ Moisture crystals, such as Soil Moist

✓ A plant that will make more from cuttings (see list)

✓ Some food coloring (optional)

✓ Water

✓ Rooting hormone

7. **Roll the stem in rooting hormone.** Follow the directions on the package. Never dip the stem directly into the package. To keep the rooting hormone pure, pour a little out onto a napkin and then throw away what's left on the napkin.

8. **Press the cutting into the gel in the glass, so the upper leaves stick out and 1–2 inches of stem are firmly in the gel.**

9. **Put your glass in a spot indoors where it gets good bright light but not full sun.** It should stay room temperature, preferably around 70 degrees. Every day check to make sure there is enough water in the glass. Your cutting has to drink water in order to root. In a week or so, you will begin to see tiny roots spread out into the gel.

10. **After a month or so, you can carefully lift the baby plant and its roots (use a spoon) and plant it into a pot with soil.** Some of the gel will cling to the roots. That's OK. Don't try to take it off. Congratulations! You've made a new plant!

Some good plants to make cuttings from:
begonias, coleus, geranium, good luck bamboo, ivy, New Guinea impatiens, *Pachysandra*, spider plant (use the babies), tomatoes.

📋 WHAT TO DO | Bulb & Pansy Planters

A fall full of beautiful flowers is fun to have! (Go ahead, try saying that three times fast!) It's even better when the flowers reappear in the spring, with a few "surprise" guests. Here's how to make it happen.

1. **Make sure there are drainage holes in the bottom of the pot.** Bulbs can't sit in water. They will rot.

2. **Line the bottom of the pot with about 1 inch of broken pottery, gravel, or packing peanuts, so you have good drainage.**

3. **Scoop 1–2 inches of soil into the pot.** You should be about 3–4 inches from the top of the pot.

📋 WHAT YOU NEED

- ✓ A plastic planting container, at least 6–8 inches wider and 6 inches deep

- ✓ Some broken pottery, gravel, or packing peanuts

- ✓ Potting soil

- ✓ 5–7 daffodil bulbs—'Tete-a-Tete' or another dwarf variety is particularly nice.

- ✓ 5–7 winter-hardy pansies from a flat or cell packs (if they are available in the fall, they are probably winter hardy)

📖 WHAT TO DO | Bulb & Pansy Planters *(continued)*

Bulb top, or "neck"

Bulb bottom

New roots

4. Arrange one layer of daffodil bulbs in the pot so that they cover the space without touching. Bulbs should go right side up (hello!), but sometimes it's hard to tell up from down. They have a bottom and a "neck," which is where the leaves were. The slightly flat side is the bottom and the tapered, cut off side is the top. Now fill in around them with soil so that the soil comes up to their "necks," and you can just barely see where they are.

5. Take the pansies out of the cell packs. Gently tease open the roots and rest them in between the bulbs, until the spaces between the bulbs are filled.

6. Fill in with soil up to the crowns of the pansies.

7. Water gently, to settle them.

8. Put your planter in a partly sunny spot outside. Watch it grow and enjoy it all fall.

9. After the first freeze, dig a hole in the ground and put your planter partway into the ground, or heap some soil around the pot. You want to protect the bulbs from hard freezing and thawing. But it must stay outside! Bulbs need the cold of winter to bloom in spring.

10. In the spring, once the daytime temperatures are above 50 degrees, when you see the pansies flowering, pull the planter out of the ground, water it with a little liquid fertilizer, and enjoy the show!

WHAT TO DO | Amaryllis Pots

An amaryllis is a great, big, fat bulb. Planting one is incredibly easy, and the fun of watching it grows never goes away. Just when the garden outside is going to sleep for the winter, an amaryllis flowering in the house always makes me smile! If you start a few of these in late October or early November, you can give them as holiday gifts!

WHAT YOU NEED

1. Amaryllis likes to be snug in its pot, so make sure the pot is only a bit wider than the bulb.

2. Put enough soil into the bottom of the pot so that the bulb will sit about half in, half out of the pot. Set the bulb on top

3. Fill around it with soil and really tuck it in, so when the bulb grows it will be snug enough to **stand up.** You may need to put three or four little chopsticks or bamboo stakes along side it as it grows taller. Amaryllis can be top heavy!

✓ An amaryllis bulb. These can be found in garden centers and fancy hardware stores from late summer to early winter. They come in many shades from white to pink to red to orange, and many shapes of flowers, so look at the picture tags and pick ones you like.

✓ A pot that is only a little tiny bit wider than the bulb itself.

✓ Potting soil

✓ A watering can with water

✓ Grass seed (if you want it) or decorative stones or moss

Ready to go!

4. **Sprinkle just a little grass around the edges, so you can have a mini-lawn to trim or to let grow wild.** You don't have to do this step, but it looks pretty and it's fun to watch the grass seed grow.

5. **Now water the whole thing well and fill in around the bulb if the soil settles.**

6. **Don't water your amaryllis too much.** The bulb will rot if it gets too wet. Let it dry out well between watering. Check it often by feeling the soil with your finger.

7. **Put it inside the house on a bright, sunny windowsill.**

8. **In a few days or weeks, you will start to see a little green sprout coming up from the center.** It will get bigger and bigger. This is the flower stalk. Just wait till you see how tall it gets and how gorgeous the flowers are!

9. **After it flowers (about 4–6 weeks after you plant it), leaves will come out on either side of the flower stalk.** Then, the flower stalk will die back. Fertilize the plant just as leaves emerge, and again when the flower stalk starts to die. Make sure it gets lots of light. When the leaves start to die, put it in a cool (50–60 degree), dark place for about 2–3 months. Then take it out and start all over again!

📋 WHAT TO DO | Halloween Hats

Here's a silly Halloween idea—go as a plant!
Here's a simple hat to make for you or maybe
a scarecrow friend. Make it a week or two
before Halloween, and then make a big show
trick-or-treating.

1. Try the hat on to make sure it fits.
2. With a sharp pair of scissors, cut off the dome of the hat about halfway up.
3. Turn it upside down and fit it back into the hat. (Yes, I know it looks silly!)
4. Staple or sew around the edge to hold it in place.
5. Soak the hat in warm water for a few minutes, then pour out the water and shake it gently.

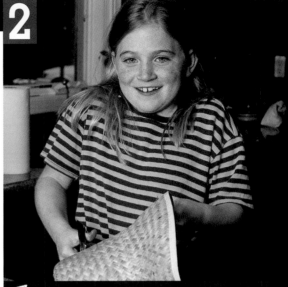

📋 WHAT YOU NEED

✓ A big straw hat from the dollar store, or a leftover hat from the summer (one with a tall crown works great)

✓ A heavy duty stapler or thick needle and thread

✓ Scissors

✓ Grass seed

✓ A plastic plant liner to fit inside the top of the hat

✓ Soil

✓ A few small plants (see list)

✓ Sheet or sphagnum moss

🪚 WHAT TO DO | Halloween Hats (continued)

6. **Press grass seed into the weave of the straw.** Try to tuck the seed in, so it doesn't fall out.

7. **Plant your plants into the plastic liner.** Since there are no drainage holes in the liner (and you don't want any unless you like the water dripping on your head), be careful not to use too much soil or to water a lot once you've planted.

8. **Use the moss to disguise the edges of the planter and to cover the surface of the soil.**

9. **Place your hat in a warm, sunny spot.** In one week to ten days the grass seed will germinate. You'll have grass growing from your hat and plants growing out of your head!

10. **You know how your parents are always telling you to stand up straight?** You'll have to stand up really straight and not bend or dip once you put your Halloween hat on or your plants will fall off. Enjoy it!

This makes a great costume, especially if you wear brown or black clothes and tape masking tape "roots" coming down from your head spreading out all over your body. Or, if you're a sloucher like I am, make a scarecrow from old clothes and give him a growing hat. Either way, this is a fun way to bring the growing season into the Halloween season!

Some fun plant ideas: pansies, mums, cat palms, peace lilies

winter
wonderlands

Garden Aquariums

Owning your own fish is a great thing, but

making him his own home is even more fun!

Create your own water garden, add a fish,

and—abracadabra!—you and your fish

can live happily ever after!

chapter 5

49

WHAT TO DO | Garden Aquariums

1. **Pour water into your container until it is full to the widest spot, but leave at least 2 inches from the top for air (and to add your fish later).**

2. **Use a scoop or spoon and evenly spread a layer of pebbles across the bottom.** Try not to let your hands touch the water. We have germs on our hands that can get into the water and are bad for fish.

3. **Nestle the bottoms of a few pieces of good luck bamboo into the pebbles so they stand on the bottom and lean against the top.** Cross the trunks in "tepee" form so your fish can swim in and out.

4. **Following the directions on the bottle, spray two or three drops of Stress Coat or other protective coating into the water.** This helps your little fish keep healthy skin even during the journey to his new home.

5. **Are you ready? In one quick move, pour the fish out of his travel bag or box into his new home.** He may look dazed or swim lopsidedly for a few minutes. Leave him and don't tap on the tank or make loud noises for a while. He needs to get his "sea legs."

6. **Once he seems calm, give him a tiny pinch of food.** Do not overfeed your fish. He will keep eating as long as there is food in his tank, and then he will get very sick. Only feed him every two or three days.

WHAT YOU NEED

✓ A clear, clean glass container that holds at least one gallon of water

✓ Enough clean pebbles or marbles to cover the bottom

✓ Three pieces of good luck bamboo tall enough to stick out of the top

✓ One gallon of water that has been allowed to sit, open air, overnight

✓ One beta or goldfish from the pet store (they are usually boy fish, just so you know)

✓ Stress Coat and fish food

7. **Watch him for as long as it takes to know his name.** It will come to you, I promise!

8. **Once a week, let a bowl of water sit overnight. In the morning, change his water.** Take the bamboo out and run it under warm water. Pour out as much of the water in his tank as you can. Pour or scoop him with a few inches of water into a clean cup or glass. Clean his tank with a soft cloth but no soap. Leftover soap in the tank can make him sick. When his tank is clean, pour in the new water, add a few squirts of Stress Coat, and then pour him back in, just as you did the first time.

9. **Never touch your fish or his water with your fingers!** It's bad for your finny friend.

Now enjoy your new companion!

WHAT TO DO | Venus Flytrap Terrariums

The word "terrarium" is Latin. It means earth-like habitat. We can create terrariums, mini environments very different from where we live, so that we can grow plants we wouldn't normally get to see. Most carnivorous (meat-eating) plants live in the rain forest, far from my house or yours. Plants that can eat meat seem to capture (get it?) the kid in all of us. Here's a great way to get to know one up close and personal.

WHAT YOU NEED

✓ A Venus flytrap plant

✓ A large, clear glass container (with a lid or cover)

✓ A cup of charcoal (from a plant, pool, or aquarium supply store)

✓ Orchid bark or a handful of dry mulch

✓ Sphagnum moss (usually the Venus flytrap is packed in it)

✓ Water

1. **Pour a cupful of charcoal into the bottom of the container.** Be careful not to breathe in while you do it or you will cough. Since your container will be closed, unlike the side of a tree, where water and debris can run off, the charcoal acts as a filter and keeps your terrarium clean and healthy.

☑ WHAT TO DO | Venus Flytrap Terrariums *(continued)*

2. **Add a cupful of bark or mulch.** Don't shake the container! You want to create layers, as if it were the trunk of a tree.

3. **Here comes the fun part! Gently take your Venus flytrap out of its pot.** Pull the moss off the roots very gently! Now have a look. Notice how thin and stringy the roots look. Have a long, close look at the mouths. Try running a pencil gently over the inside hairs. Does the mouth close? If so, then it may be hungry.

4. **Pull the moss off the plant and sprinkle it into your container.** You should now have three layers: charcoal, bark and moss. These will act like the tree trunk and decomposing leaves. Your plant should feel right at home.

5. **Poke a hole into the center of the moss with your finger and set the Venus flytrap into the hole.**

6. **Gently pour a cup of water over the plant.** Water should come up to just where the charcoal and the bark meet, not any higher. Always keep water in your terrarium at about that level. It will keep your terrarium humid, just like the rainforest, without drowning your plant.

7. **Put the lid or cover on your new Venus flytrap terrarium.**

8. **Stand in the middle of the room with your hands stretched up in the air.** (Yes, really, I know it's silly—just do it!) How often do you think a fly will land right in the middle of one of your hands? Right, about once a month. That is as often as you should feed your plant. When you do feed it, place a tiny, fly-sized piece of any uncooked meat into one mouth. Only feed one mouth every month or so. Feeding more often will kill your plant. You don't have to feed it meat. You can give it a very light dose of liquid fertilizer every month or so instead.

Your terrarium needs to be in a light, but not sunny spot. Too much sun will fry it. Water only when the level gets below the charcoal. Enjoy your ghoulish guest! *continued on page 56* ▶

Cool Facts

Venus flytraps live in the rain forest high up in the trees. Their seeds land in the crooks of trees and the plants grow there, tucked into the branches. They've learned to live on mostly water, clinging to the bark of the trees. Venus flytraps had to find another way to get the nutrients that most plants get from the soil through their roots. That's why they "eat" bugs.

Take a look at the roots when you plant your Venus flytrap. They are very small and puny in comparison to most regular plants. That's because most plants' roots do all the work of absorbing water and nutrients from the soil. Because Venus flytraps don't live in soil, they've adapted differently. All their roots really do is steady them against a tree, like an anchor.

Look deep into the open "mouth" of a Venus flytrap. The mouths are specially formed leaves. They photosynthesize, which means they make food from sunlight, but these wide leaves with what looks like eyelashes also collect the minerals the plant needs to survive. Here's how. Do you see little tiny hairs standing up inside the mouth? They are the triggers. If you poke the eyelashes of the plant, nothing will happen. But if you brush those hairs with a pencil tip or finger the plant just may gently, quickly close. (If it's not "hungry," it won't close. Venus flytraps don't waste food.)

The plant holds its prey while it absorbs the liquids of the trapped.
This is how it has adapted to get the minerals it needs.
How gross is that?

📋 WHAT TO DO | Sand Art Terrariums

The great thing about our planet is that there are all different kinds of places, with all different kinds of weather and plants. This pretty little terrarium is for completely different plants than the Venus flytrap terrarium. It's a lot of fun to make and then a beauty to have around the house!

1. Soak the peat pellet in warm water until it's fully soft and expanded.
2. Set it into the bottom of the container.
3. Use the pellet as a guide and fill around it with colored sand. Make patterns with the sand. You can put a stick down the sides to make even more patterns.

📋 WHAT YOU NEED

- ✓ A tall, straight sided container
- ✓ One peat pellet
- ✓ Colored sand (from a craft store)
- ✓ Potting soil
- ✓ A few small tropical plants (see list)
- ✓ Water

WHAT TO DO | Sand Art Terrariums *(continued)*

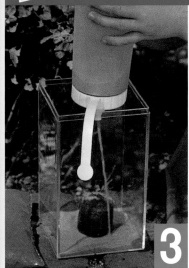

4. Now cover the sand with a layer at least 2 inches deep of potting soil.

5. Decide what plants you want in your terrarium and set them, in their pots, on the soil. Do they look nice? Move them around until you're happy with the way they look.

6. Now gently turn the pots upside down into your hand and coax the plants out of their pots. Tease the roots open and set each plant onto the soil.

7. Fill in around the plants with soil, tucking it in with your fingers.

8. Water with a cup or so of warm water. You can tell how much water is in the terrarium by holding it up high and looking at the sides and bottom. If water comes up through the sand, you've watered too much. Leave it for as many days as it takes for the water to be used up, then be sure to water less the next time.

9. Keep your terrarium inside in a mostly bright to sunny spot. Watch it to see how often it needs to be watered.

10. Enjoy your terrarium!

🔍 MORE ABOUT SAND ART TERRARIUMS

Plants

Here are some good plants for your tropical terrarium. Most can be found at a good local garden center. Make sure they look healthy and happy when you buy them!

- Coral berry
- Belgian evergreen
- Dwarf creeping fig
- Mosaic plant
- Aluminum plant
- Table ferns
- Miniature African violets
- Club moss, fern moss
- Arrowhead vine, (*Nephthytis*)
- Polka dot plant
- Snake plant

African Violets

Polka dot plant

📋 WHAT TO DO | Succulent Gardens

Succulents are the desert plants that have fat fleshy leaves but no prickles, like a cactus has. They're a great way to grow a desert garden without hurting yourself.

1. Put the pottery or peanuts in the bottom of the pot so the drainage holes don't become blocked.
2. Fill the container halfway with potting soil. Pat it down with your fingers so it is flat.
3. Set the succulent plants, still in their pots, into the container, then move them around until you like the way they look.
4. Now gently turn each pot upside down into your hand and squeeze or tap the pot so the plant slides into your hand. Set it right side up in the place it belongs. Don't bury the plants, just set them on the bed of soil. Don't worry if they fall over a little. Do this with each plant. If the roots are tightly packed in a ball, gently tease the roots apart with your fingers so they spread out into the container.

📋 WHAT YOU NEED

✓ A wide shallow dish or bulb pan with good drainage

✓ Broken pottery or foam peanuts for drainage

✓ Potting soil

✓ Clean decorative sand (store-bought sand, not from the beach because salt can kill plants)

✓ A few succulent plants (see list)

WHAT TO DO | Succulent Gardens *(continued)*

5. **Pour sand around the plants.** Stand them up and settle them in as needed. Don't cover them, just fill in with sand to the level where the roots and stems meet (the crown).

6. Fill a cup with water and very gently pour water, like a soft rain, over the fingers of one hand so you are watering enough to soak the roots but not make a hole in the sand or overwater the plants.

7. **Place your garden in a bright sunny spot in the house.** The more sun it gets, the happier it will be. Think desert!

8. **The rule of thumb is to water your plants every time it rains in Arizona.** Since that's not always easy to follow, watch your plants carefully. Water once a week or less, depending on how happy they look.

These sturdy little gardens will last for years with almost no care on your part. They're a great low-maintenance gift for a sick friend or an older relative with a sunny apartment.

Plants

Here are some good plants for a desert garden:

Aloe   Living stone

Blue jewel   Peperomia

Ghost plant   Sempervivum

Haworthia   Sedum

Jade

Living Stone

Haworthia

Aloe

Sempervivum
(hen and chicks)

and one to grow on

chapter 6

Stepping Stones

This project should be done with a grown-up. So don't make just one—let them do one too. It creates a memory to last a lifetime! Make these as birthday gifts, for a birthday party or a family reunion, for Christmas for your grandparents . . . anytime you want to make a lasting memory. Be creative, and have fun!

📋 WHAT TO DO | Stepping Stones

1. Set the pizza box on a flat surface outside where it can sit for the next three days.

2. **Following the instructions on the bag of mortar mix, mix the mortar in the plastic bucket.** Mix it as dry as possible and add water as needed to make a stiff but pliable mixture. Use the mixing stick to really stir it well, so there are no powder pockets. Let it sit for 2–3 minutes after mixing to see if water rises to the surface or if it feels too stiff. Adjust as needed. Use about 10 pounds of mix per stepping stone. (It must be at least 2–2½ inches deep in the box.) Have the grown-up do this. It's hard work, and you must keep the mix away from your face.

3. **Pour the prepared, wet mix into the box and smooth it out with your hands or mixing paddle.** If the mix is too wet, you can soak up a little water on top with some paper towels. If it's really too wet or too runny, pour it back into the bucket, add more dry mix, and try again.

4. ***Don't get the concrete in your face!*** Keep your hands away from your face while you are making your stepping stone.

📋 WHAT YOU NEED

✓ A cardboard pizza or carry-out box, about 10 x 10 inches

✓ A large plastic bucket with a lid (a 5-gallon paint bucket works great)

✓ Sakrete mortar mix (the smoothest blend possible)

✓ Water

✓ A big mixing paddle (a large-sized paint mixer is great)

✓ Shells, stones, mosaic tiles, or memorabilia you want to "set in stone"

✓ A sharp stick or knife

✓ Paper towel and handy wipes

✓ A flat surface

✓ Soap and water to wash up!

5. **To make a handprint, spread your hand out wide and press it, palm down, into the concrete.** Jiggle your hand slightly, as you would wiggle your toes down into the sand at the beach. Get each of your fingers at least halfway into the mix. Then lift your hand straight out without twisting it. You should have a nice clean print. If not, do it again right away.

6. **To write, use a sharp stick or a knife.** Cut each letter in then wiggle to the sides to make the letters wide. Or press in stones or twigs to form letters and numbers.

7. **If you want to add any stones, shells, tiles, or toys, press them down hard so that they make good contact with the wet concrete.**

8. ***Go and wash your hands immediately,*** with lots of soap and water. Concrete has chemicals in it that should not stay on your hands. Dry them off well. Do this as soon as you finish! If you want to use the bucket again, wash it out immediately or it will harden. But *don't* pour the concrete water down a drain. You will ruin your plumbing!

9. **When you are finished, leave the stepping stone right where it is for the next three days.** Don't move it or it might crack! After three days it will be fully dry and ready to move.

10. **After three days, rip the box off, and you're ready to give it to someone you love!**

some last words

If insects or disease is a problem, don't give up! There are plenty of people who want to help you be a successful gardener. Two places to get help are at your local extension service and garden centers. To find your local extension service, look online or in the phone book.

Finding a helpful garden center isn't hard either. Ask anyone you know who gardens or look in the phone book.

If you have used soil that you want to use again, you can, but you might want to "cook" it first. Put a one-inch layer of soil on a baking sheet or cookie tray. Turn the oven on to 250 degrees and cook the soil for one hour. This will kill any bacteria or insects lurking in the soil and make it safe (once it's cooled down) to use again.

If you have questions or comments on these projects, please feel free to email me at CKKrezel@yahoo.com. Or you and a parent can visit these good Web sites to learn more about gardening:
American Horticultural Society,
www.ahs.org
Gardener's Net,
www.gardenersnet.com
National Gardening Association,
www.nationalgardening.com
The Succulent Plant Page,
www.succulent-plant.com

I hope that you have as much fun with these projects as I have had. Happy gardening!

Analogous colors. Colors on opposite sides of the color wheel, creating high contrast

Aquarium. A container that recreates a water environment

Carnivorous. Meat-eating

Cell pack. The small plastic containers in which plants are sold in spring, usually 4–8 per pack.

Clitellum. The soft "ring" on a worm in which it carries its eggs

Complementary colors. Colors that are similar and blend into one another

Compost. Decayed organic matter, high in nutrients, used in the garden

Condensation. The liquid formed on a surface when moisture is released from the air, as it turns from a gas to a liquid state

Crown of the plant. The place where the roots and stem meet

Ectothermic. Cold-blooded, needing the warmth of the sun to stimulate circulation, like frogs and butterflies.

Monochromatic. Using all one color, as in an all-white garden

Organic. Having no chemicals, natural

Peat moss. A spongy substance used as a planting material

Peat pellets. Peat, sold compressed and netted, which when soaked, swells up to form planting pellets

Photosynthesis. The conversion of light energy into chemical energy done by plants, usually by the leaves. It's how plants "eat."

Terrarium. A container that recreates one of earth's land environments

about the author

Cindy Krezel is a nursery professional and author. Her articles have appeared in the *New York Times*, *Newsday*, and *American Nurseryman* magazine, and on numerous Web sites. For twelve years she was the Education Coordinator at Martin Viette Nurseries, a prestigious Long Island garden center. She is currently Director of Development for Planting Fields Foundation at Planting Fields Arboretum State Historic Park. Her spare time goes to Plant A Row for the Hungry and The Interfaith Nutrition Network, the largest provider of food and social services to the hungry and homeless on Long Island.

72